CONTENTS

4

43

2

14

24

32

18

BE-LEAF IT MUG RUG

MEASUREMENTS

Approx 5 x 7½"/12.5 x 19cm

MATERIALS

Yarn

Lily® Sugar'n Cream®, 2½oz/70.9g skeins, each approx 120yd/109m (cotton)
•1 skein each of #00016 Dark Pine or #01712 Hot Green

Needles

• Size 7 (4.5 mm) knitting needles, *or size needed to obtain gauge*

Notions

• 2 stitch markers

GAUGE

20 sts and 30 rows = 4"/10cm in garter st using size 7 (4.5mm) needles. *TAKE TIME TO CHECK GAUGE.*

INSTRUCTIONS

Cast on 3 sts.

1st row: K1. PM. K1. PM. K1.

2nd row: Knit to marker. yo. SM. K1. SM. yo. Knit to end of row. Rep 2nd row until there are 25 sts on needle.

Next row: K1. K2tog. Knit to marker. yo. SM. K1. SM. yo. Knit to last 3 sts. K2tog. K1.

Next row: Knit.

Rep last 2 rows twice more.

Knit 4 rows (garter st).

Next row: K1. K2tog. Knit to end of row.

Next row: Knit.

Next row: Knit to last 3 sts. K2tog. K1.

Next row: Knit.

Rep last 4 rows until 3 sts rem.

Next row: K3tog.

FINISHING

Cast off.•

EVERYBODY KNIT HAT

Easy

SIZES

To fit 2/4 yrs (5/7 yrs, Adult)

MATERIALS

Yarn

Caron® Simply Soft®, 6oz/170.1g skeins, each approx 315yd/288m (acrylic)
• 1 (1, 1) skein each #39762 Burgundy, #39765 Pumpkin or #39782 Gold

Needles

• Set of 4 size 8 (5mm) double-pointed knitting needles, *or size needed to obtain gauge*

Notion

• Stitch marker

GAUGE

18 sts and 24 rows = 4"/10cm in stockinette st. using size 8 (5mm) needles. *TAKE TIME TO CHECK GAUGE.*

HAT

Cast on 72 (80, 88) sts. Divide sts onto 3 needles and join in rnd, taking care not to twist the sts, and placing marker on first st.

1st rnd: *(K1tbl) twice. (P1tbl) twice. Rep from * around.

Rep last rnd until work from beg measures 6½ (7½, 8½)"/16.5 (19, 21.5)cm.

Shape Crown

1st rnd: *(K1tbl) twice. P2tog. Rep from * around. 54 (60, 66) sts.

2nd to 4th rnds: *(K1tbl) twice. P1tbl. Rep from * around.

5th rnd: *K2tog. P1tbl. ssk. P1tbl. Rep from * around. 36 (40, 44) sts.

6th rnd: *K1tbl. P1tbl. Rep from * around.

7th rnd: *K2tog. ssk. Rep from * around. 18 (20, 22) sts.

8th rnd: *K2tog. Rep from * around. 9 (10, 11) sts.

FINISHING

Break yarn, leaving a long end. Thread end through rem sts and fasten securely.•

FINGERLESS GLOVES

Intermediate

SIZES
Adult S/M (L/XL)

MATERIALS

Yarn 🔢
Patons® Classic Wool Worsted™, 3½oz/100g skeins, each approx. 210yd/192m (wool)
• 1 (1) skein #77747 Claret

Needles
• Set of 4 size 5 (3.75mm) double-pointed knitting needles, *or size needed to obtain gauge*
• Set of 6 (4mm) double-pointed knitting needles

Notions
• Stitch marker
• Safety pin

GAUGE
22 sts and 28 rows = 4"/10cm using larger needles in stockinette st. *TAKE TIME TO CHECK GAUGE.*

GLOVES

Right Glove
**With set of smaller double-pointed needles, cast on 42 (48) sts. Divide sts evenly on 3 needles, having 14 (16) sts on each needle. Join in rnd, taking care not to twist the sts. PM on first st.
1st rnd: *K1tbl. P1. Rep from * around.
Rep last rnd of (K1tbl. P1) ribbing for 4"/10cm.
Change to larger set of needles and knit 7 rnds.**

Shape thumb gusset
1st rnd: K22 (25). (Kfb) twice. Knit to end of rnd. 44 (50) sts.
2nd and alt rnds: Knit.
3rd rnd: K22 (25). Kfb. K2. Kfb. Knit to end of rnd. 46 (52) sts.
5th rnd: K22 (25). Kfb. K4. Kfb. Knit to end of rnd. 48 (54) sts.
7th rnd: K22 (25). Kfb. K6. Kfb. Knit to end of rnd. 50 (56) sts.
9th rnd: K22 (25). Kfb. K8. Kfb. Knit to end of rnd. 52 (58) sts.
11th rnd: K22 (25). Kfb. K10. Kfb. Knit to end of rnd. 54 (60) sts.
13th rnd: K36 (39). Slip last 14 sts onto safety pin (thumb opening). Knit to end of rnd.
****14th rnd:** Knit to end of rnd, casting on 2 sts over slipped sts. 42 (48) sts.
Knit in rnds until work after ribbing measures 4 (4½)"/10 (11.5)cm, dec 2 sts evenly across last rnd. 40 (46) sts.
Next rnd: *K1tbl. P1. Rep from * around.
Rep last rnd of (K1tbl. P1) ribbing for 1½ (2)"/4 (5)cm. Cast off in ribbing.

Thumb
With RS facing, join yarn to base of thumb, pick up and knit 2 sts. K14 from safety pin. Divide these 16 sts onto 3 needles (5, 5, 6).
Work 3 rnds of (K1tbl. P1) ribbing. Cast off in ribbing.***

Left Glove

Work from ** to ** as given for Right Glove.

Shape thumb gusset

1st rnd: K18 (21). (Kfb) twice. Knit to end of rnd. 44 (50) sts.

2nd and alt rnds: Knit.

3rd rnd: K18 (21). Kfb. K2. Kfb. Knit to end of rnd. 46 (52) sts.

5th rnd: K18 (21). Kfb. K4. Kfb. Knit to end of rnd. 48 (54) sts.

7th rnd: K18 (21). Kfb. K6. Kfb. Knit to end of rnd. 50 (56) sts.

9th rnd: K18 (21). Kfb. K8. Kfb. Knit to end of rnd. 52 (58) sts.

11th rnd: K18 (21). Kfb. K10. Kfb. Knit to end of rnd. 54 (60) sts.

13th rnd: K32 (35). Slip last 14 sts onto safety pin (thumb opening). Knit to end of rnd.

Work from *** to *** as given for Right Glove.

FINISHING

Cut yarn after binding off and weave in ends.•

IRISH MOSS FLOOR PILLOW

Basic

MEASUREMENT

Approx 30"/76cm square

MATERIALS

Yarn 🔢

Patons® Cobbles™, 3.5oz/100g skeins, each approx.
41yd/37m (wool/acrylic/nylon)

• 11 skeins #85315 Frosted Plum

Needles

• Size 17 (12.75mm) knitting needles, *or size needed to obtain gauge*

Notion

• 30"/76cm square pillow form

GAUGE

6½ sts and 8 rows = 4"/10cm in Irish Moss Pat using size 17 (12.75mm) needles. *TAKE TIME TO CHECK GAUGE.*

PILLOW (Make 2 pieces alike)

Cast on 50 sts.

1st row (RS): *K1. P1. Rep from * to end of row.

2nd row: As 1st row.

3rd row: *P1. K1. Rep from * to end of row.

4th row: As 3rd row.

These 4 rows form Irish Moss Pattern (Pat).

Cont in Irish Moss Pat until work from beg measures approx 30"/76cm, ending on a 4th row of pat. Cast off.

FINISHING

Pin pieces to measurements. Cover with a damp cloth, leaving cloth to dry.

Sew 3 sides of Pillow together. Insert pillow form. Sew opening closed.•

PLANT COZIES

Easy

MEASUREMENTS
To fit plant pot 6"/15cm diameter x 6"/15cm high.

MATERIALS
Yarn 🔵
Patons® Classic Wool Roving™, 3½oz/100g skeins, each approx 120yd/109m (wool)
• 1 skein in #77420 Pale Blush or #77309 Frosted Plum or #77010 Natural or #77044 Grey

Needles
• Size U.S.10 (6mm) knitting needles, *or size needed to obtain gauge*

GAUGE
15 sts and 20 rows = 4"/10cm in stockinette st using size 10 (6mm) needles. *TAKE TIME TO CHECK GAUGE.*

PLANT COZIES
Beg at top edge, cast on 60 sts.
1st row (RS): *K1. P1. Rep from * to end of row.
2nd row: *P1. K1. Rep from * to end of row.
Rep last 2 rows Seed St Pat once more, then 2nd row once.

Next row (WS): K1. *K1. yo. Sl1P. Rep from * to last st. K1.
Next row: Sl1P. K1. *Sl1P (the yo). K2. Rep from * to end of row.
Proceed in pat as follows:
1st row (WS): Sl1P. *yo. Sl1P. K2tog (yo and next st). Rep from * to last st. K1.
2nd row: Sl1P. *K2. Sl1P (the yo). Rep from * to last st. K1.
3rd row: Sl1P. *K2tog (yo and next st). yo. Sl1P. Rep from * to last st. K1.
4th row: Sl1P. K1. *Sl1P (the yo). K2. Rep from * to end of row. These 4 rows form pat.

Cont even in pat until piece measures 5"/12.5cm or approx 1"/2.5cm shorter than desired length to cover your plant pot, ending on a 3rd row of pat.
Next row (RS): *K1. K2tog (yo and next st). Rep from * to last 2 sts. K2. 60 sts
Next row: Purl.
Next row: *K6. K2tog. Rep from * to last 4 sts. K4. 53 sts. Cast off knitwise (WS).

FINISHING
Sew side seam.•

BOTH SIDES NOW SCARF

Intermediate

MEASUREMENTS

Approx 6½ x 72"/16.5 x 183cm

MATERIALS

Yarn ⑤

Patons® Alpaca Blend™, 3½oz/100 skeins, each approx 155yd/142m (acrylic/wool/nylon/alpaca)

• 4 skeins in #01016 Petunia

Needles

• Size 10 (6mm) knitting needles, *or size needed to obtain gauge*

Notion

• Cable needle

GAUGE

15 sts and 20 rows = 4"/10cm in stockinette st using size 10 (6mm) needles. *TAKE TIME TO CHECK GAUGE.*

INSTRUCTIONS

Note: Scarf is reversible.

Cast on 48 sts.

1st row: (RS) (K1. P1) 24 times.

2nd and alt rows: (K1. P1) 24 times.

3rd and 5th rows: As 1st row.

7th row: *Slip 8 sts onto cable needle and leave at back of work. (K1. P1) 4 times. (K1. P1) 4 times from cable needle. (K1. P1) 4 times. Rep from * once more.

9th, 11th, 13th and 15th rows: As 1st row.

17th row: *(K1. P1) 4 times. Slip 8 sts onto cable needle and leave at front of work. (K1. P1) 4 times. (K1. P1) 4 times from cable needle. Rep from * once more.

19th row: As 1st row.

20th row: As 2nd row.

Rep last 20 rows until work from beg measures approx 72"/183cm, ending on a 15th row.

FINISHING

Cast off in pat.•

SAMPLER AFGHAN

MEASUREMENTS

Approx 48" x 60"/122cm x 152.5cm

MATERIALS

Yarn

Caron® One Pound™, 16oz/453.6g skeins, each approx 812yd/742m (acrylic)
• 1 skein each in #10585 Lace (A), #10514 Off White (B), and #10617 Medium Gray Mix (C)

Needles
• Size 8 (5mm) knitting needles, *or size needed to obtain gauge*

GAUGES

• 15 sts and 22 rows = 4"/10cm in Basket Weave Pat. using size 8 (5mm) needles.
• 20 sts and 20 rows = 4"/10cm in Trinity St Pat. using size 8 (5mm) needles.
• 17 sts and 20 rows = 4"/10cm in Mock Cable Pat. using size 8 (5mm) needles.
TAKE TIME TO CHECK GAUGES.

AFGHAN

Block I (make 7)

With A, cast on 45 sts.

1st row (RS): Knit.

2nd row: K5. *P3. K5. Rep from * to end of row.

3rd row: P5. *K3. P5. Rep from * to end of row.

4th row: As 2nd row.

5th row: Knit.

6th row: K1. P3. *K5. P3. Rep from * to last st. K1.

7th row: P1. K3. *P5. K3. Rep from * to last st. P1.

8th row: As 6th row.

These 8 rows form Basket Weave Pat.

Cont in pat until work from beg measures approx 12"/30.5cm, ending on a 1st or 5th row. Cast off knitwise (WS).

Block II (make 7)

With B, cast on 52 sts.

1st row (RS): Purl.

2nd row: Knit, inc 10 sts evenly across. 62 sts.

Proceed in Trinity St Pat.

1st row (RS): Purl.

2nd row: K1. *(K1. P1. K1) all in next st. P3tog. Rep from * to last st. K1.

3rd row: Purl.

4th row: K1. *P3tog. (K1. P1. K1) all in next st. Rep from * to last st. K1.

These 4 rows form Trinity St Pat.

Cont in pat until work from beg measures approx 11¾"/30cm, ending on a RS row.

Next row: Knit, dec 10 sts evenly across. 52 sts.

Next row: Purl.

Cast off knitwise (WS).

Block III (make 6)

With C, cast on 52 sts.

1st row (WS): *K2. P3. Rep from * to last 2 sts. K2.

2nd row: *P2. Sl1. K2. psso 2 knit sts. Rep from * to last 2 sts. P2.

3rd row: *K2. P1. yo. P1. Rep from * to last 2 sts. K2.

4th row: *P2. K3. Rep from * to last 2 sts. P2.

These 4 rows form Mock Cable Pat.

Cont in pat until work from beg measures 12"/30.5cm, ending on a 4th row. Cast off knitwise (WS).

FINISHING

Following Assembly Diagram, sew Blocks tog.●

I	III	II	I
II	I	III	II
III	II	I	III
I	III	II	I
II	I	III	II

COFFEE PRESS & MUG COZIES

Easy

MEASUREMENTS

To fit Coffee Press approx 7"/18cm tall, 12"/30.5cm around

To fit Mug approx 4"/10cm tall x 10¼"/26cm around

MATERIALS

Yarn

Caron® Simply Soft® 6oz/170g skeins, each approx 315yd/288m (acrylic)

• 1 skein in #39765 Pumpkin

Note: 1 skein will make 4 Coffee Press Cozies or 9 Mug Cozies.

Needles and Hooks

• Size 8 (5mm) knitting needles, *or size needed to obtain gauge*

• Size H/8 (5mm) crochet hook for ties for Mug Cozy

Notions

• 3 stitch markers

• 6 buttons medium size (approx ¾"/2cm) for Coffee Press Cozy

• 3 buttons small size (approx ½"/1.5cm) for Mug Cozy

GAUGE

18 sts and 24 rows = 4"/10cm in stockinette st using size 8 (5mm) needles. *TAKE TIME TO CHECK GAUGE.*

COFFEE PRESS COZY

Cast on 50 sts.

1st row (RS): K2. *K2. P2. Rep from * to last 4 sts. K4.

2nd row: K2. *P2. K2. Rep from * to end of row.

3rd row: K2. *K2tog. Leave sts on left-hand needle. Knit first st again. Slip 2 sts off left-hand needle—cable made. P2. Rep from * to last 4 sts. Cable. K2.

4th row: As 2nd row.

Rep last 4 rows for Cable Pat until work from beg measures approx 6½"/16.5cm, ending on a 3rd row. Cast off.

Button Tabs (Make 3)

Cast on 11 sts.

1st row (WS): Knit.

2nd row (Buttonhole row): K2. yo. K2tog. Knit to last 4 sts. K2tog. yo. K2.

Knit 2 rows. Cast off (WS).

Place markers for 3 button tabs as follows:

1st at top, 2nd at bottom and last spaced evenly between. Sew buttons to correspond to buttonholes.

MUG COZY

Left Front and Back

With pair of needles, cast on 30 sts.

Work in Cable Pat as given for Coffee Press Cozy until work from beg measures approx 3¾"/9.5cm, ending on a 4th row.

Cast off.

Right Front

With pair of needles, cast on 14 sts.

Work in Cable Pat as given for Coffee Press Cozy until work from beg measures approx 3¾"/9.5cm, ending on a 4th row.

Cast off.

FINISHING

Sew Left Front and Right Front tog, securing with 3 buttons spaced evenly between.

Ties (Make 6)

With crochet hook, ch 12. Fasten off.

Sew one tie to each corner of Back. Sew third tie spaced evenly between two ties.

Rep for Right Front.

Sew 3 ties to each side spaced evenly between.•

DOG SWEATER

Intermediate

SIZES

S (M, L, XL).

MEASUREMENTS

To fit chest measurement 12 (15,18, 22)"/30.5 (38, 45.5, 56)cm

Finished chest measurement 13 (16, 19, 23.5)"/33 (40.5, 48, 59.5)cm

MATERIALS

Yarn (4)

Bernat® Super Value™, 7oz/197g skeins, each approx 440yd/402m (acrylic)

- 1 (1,1, 2) skeins in #53044 True Gray (MC)
- 1 (1, 1, 1) skein in #07407 Winter White (A)
- 1 (1, 1, 1) skein in #00607 Berry (B)

Needles

- Set of 4 size 8 (5mm) double-pointed knitting needles
- Size 8 (5mm) circular knitting needle, 16"/40.5cm long, *or size needed to obtain gauge*

Notions

- 2 stitch holders
- Stitch marker

GAUGE

18 sts and 24 rows = 4"/10cm in stockinette st using size 8 (5mm) needles.

TAKE TIME TO CHECK GAUGE.

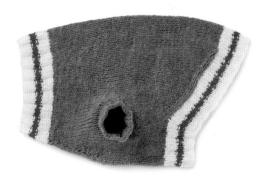

SWEATER

Note: Transfer sts from double-pointed needles to circular needle when necessary.

With double-pointed needles and A, cast on 44 (56, 68, 80) sts. Divide sts onto 3 needles. Join in rnd, placing marker on first st.

Ribbing

1st rnd (RS): *K2. P2. Rep from * around.

Rep last rnd (K2. P2) ribbing 5 times more.

Break A. Join B.

With B, rep last rnd 3 times more. Break B. Join A.

With A, rep last rnd 6 times more.

Break A. Join MC.

Next rnd: *K11 (14, 17, 20). M1. Rep from * around. 48 (60, 72, 84) sts.

Body

1st and 2nd rnds: Knit.

3rd rnd: K1. M1. Knit to last st. M1. K1. 50 (62, 74, 86) sts.

Rep these 3 rnds 4 (5, 6, 10) times more. 58 (72, 86, 106) sts.**

Knit 4 (6, 6, 10) rnds even.

Leg Openings

1st rnd: K5 (8, 10, 12). Cast off 7 (9, 10, 12) sts loosely. Knit to last 12 (17, 20, 24) sts. Cast off 7 (9, 10, 12) sts loosely. Knit to end of rnd.

2nd rnd: Knit, casting on 7 (9, 10, 12) sts over cast off sts.

Knit even until work from last rnd of ribbing measures 5 (7, 9, 12)"/12.5 (18, 23, 30.5)cm.

Back Shaping

1st rnd: Knit to last 6 (8, 12, 16) sts. Place last 6 (8, 12, 16) sts and first 6 (8, 12, 16) of next rnd onto st holder. 46 (56, 62, 74) sts.

DOG SWEATER

Purl 1 row. Working back and forth across needles in rows, proceed as follows:

1st row (RS): K2. ssk. Knit to last 4 sts. K2tog. K2. 44 (54, 60, 72) sts.

2nd row: Purl.

Rep last 2 rows 3 (4, 4, 8) times more. 38 (46, 52, 56) sts.

1st row (RS): K2. ssk. Knit to last 4 sts. K2tog. K2. 36 (44, 50, 54) sts.

2nd row: P2. P2togtbl. Purl to last 4 sts. P2tog. P2. 34 (42, 48, 52) sts.

Rep last 2 rows 4 (5, 6, 6) times more. 18 (22, 24, 28) sts. Leave sts on needle. Break MC.

FINISHING

Coat Edging

With RS facing and A, pick up and knit 15 (19, 22, 28) sts along right edge of Coat. K12 (16, 24, 32) from st holder. Pick up and knit 15 (19, 22, 28) sts along left edge of Coat. Knit rem 18 (22, 24, 28) sts on needle. Join in rnd, placing marker on first st. 60 (76, 92, 116) sts.

1st rnd: *K2. P2. Rep from * around.

Rep last rnd of (K2. P2) ribbing 3 (4, 5, 7) times more. Break A. Join B.

With B, rep last rnd 2 (3, 3, 4) times more. Break B. Join A.

With A, rep last rnd 4 (5, 6, 8) times more.

Cast off in (K2. P2) ribbing.

Leg Edging

With RS facing, MC, and double-pointed needles, pick up and knit 16 (20, 24, 28) sts around leg opening. Divide sts onto 3 needles. Join in rnd, placing marker on first st.

1st rnd: *K2. P2. Rep from * around.

Rep last rnd until Leg Edging measures 1½ (2, 2, 3)"/4 (5, 5, 7.5)cm. Cast off in (K2. P2) ribbing.•

FOR SCARF PATTERN, SEE PAGES 26-27.

ESSENTIAL STRIPES KNIT BLANKET

Easy

MEASUREMENTS

Approx 52 x 62½"/132 x 158.5cm.

MATERIALS

Yarn

Caron® One Pound™, 16oz/453.6g skeins, each approx. 812 yd/742m (acrylic)

• 1 skein each in #10514 Off White (A) and #10618 Dark Grey Mix (B)

• 2 skeins in #10616 Soft Grey Mix (C)

Needles

• Size 8 (5mm) knitting needles, *or size needed to obtain gauge*

GAUGE

13½ sts and 24 rows = 4"/10cm in garter stitch using size 8 (5mm) needles.

TAKE TIME TO CHECK GAUGE.

BLANKET

Note: Blanket is made in 5 separate Strips.

Strip 1

With C, cast on 28 sts. Work in garter st (knit every row) until work from beg measures 11"/28cm, noting first row is RS and ending on a WS row.

Next 2 rows: With B, knit.

Next 2 rows: With A, knit.

Rep last 4 rows until work from beg measures 32"/81.5cm, ending on a WS row.

With B, cont in garter st until work from beg measures 38"/96.5cm, ending on a WS row.

With A, cont in garter st until work from beg measures 52"/132cm, ending on a RS row. Cast off (WS).

Strip 2

With B, cast on 56 sts. Work in garter st (knit every row) until work from beg measures 6"/15cm, noting first row is RS and ending on a WS row.

Next 2 rows: With C, knit.

Next 2 rows: With B, knit.

Rep last 4 rows until work from beg measures 20"/51cm, ending on a WS row. With C, cont in garter st until work from beg measures 42½"/108cm, ending on a WS row.

Next 2 rows: With A, knit.

Next 2 rows: With C, knit.

Rep last 4 rows until work from beg measures 52"/132cm, ending on a RS row. Cast off (WS).

Strip 3

With A, cast on 28 sts. Work in garter st (knit every row) until work from beg measures 24"/61cm, noting first row is RS and ending on a WS row.

Next 2 rows: With B, knit.

Next 2 rows: With A, knit. Rep last 4 rows until work from beg measures 30"/76cm, ending on a WS row.

With B, cont in garter st until work from beg measures 44"/112cm, ending on a WS row.

Next 2 rows: With C, knit.

ESSENTIAL STRIPES KNIT BLANKET

Next 2 rows: With B, knit.

Rep last 4 rows until work from beg measures 52"/132cm, ending on a RS row. Cast off (WS).

Strip 4

With A, cast on 46 sts.

Next 2 rows: With A, knit.

Next 2 rows: With B, knit.

Rep last 4 rows until work from beg measures 13"/33cm, ending on a WS row.

With C, cont in garter st until work from beg measures 33"/84cm, ending on a WS row.

Next 2 rows: With A, knit.

Next 2 rows: With C, knit.

Rep last 4 rows until work from beg measures 45"/114½cm, ending on a WS row.

With A, cont in garter st until work from beg measures 52"/132cm, ending on a RS row. Cast off (WS).

Strip 5

With C, cast on 52 sts.

Next 2 rows: With C, knit.

Next 2 rows: With B, knit.

Rep last 4 rows until work from beg measures 20"/51cm, ending on a WS row.

With B, cont in garter st until work from beg measures 26½"/67.5cm, ending on a WS row.

With A, cont in garter st until work from beg measures 38½"/98cm, ending on a WS row.

Next 2 rows: With C, knit.

Next 2 rows: With B, knit.

Rep last 4 rows until work from beg measures 52"/132cm, ending on a RS row. Cast off (WS).

FINISHING

Sew Strips tog in the following order: 1, 2, 3, 4, 5. •

SPLIT RIB COWL

Easy

MEASUREMENTS

Approx 32"/81.5cm around x 24"/61cm deep

MATERIALS

Yarn (5)

Patons® Classic Wool Roving™, 3½oz/100g skeins, each approx 120yd/109m (wool)

• 4 skeins in #77219 Low Tide (MC)
• 1 skein in #77615 Yellow (A)

Needles

• Size 10 (6mm) circular knitting needle 29"/75cm long, *or size needed to obtain gauge*
• Pair of size 10 (6mm) double-pointed knitting needles

Notion

• Stitch marker

GAUGE

13 sts and 28 rows = 4"/10cm in Rib Pat using size 10 (6mm) needles.

TAKE TIME TO CHECK GAUGE.

COWL

With MC, cast on 105 sts. Do not join. Working back and forth across needle in rows, proceed as follows:

1st row: Knit.

2nd row: *P1. K1below. Rep from * to last st. P1.

Rep last 2 rows for Rib Pat until work from beg measures 8"[20.5 cm].

Next row: Knit to last 2 sts. K2tog. 104 sts. Join to work in rnd. Do not turn. Place marker on first st of rnd.

Next rnd: *K1. P1below. Rep from * around.

Next rnd: Knit.

Rep last 2 rnds for Rib Pat until work from beg measures 24"/61cm.

Cast off knitwise.

Top Edge Applied I-Cord

With MC and pair of double-pointed needles, cast on 3 sts onto right-hand needle. Beg at back of Cowl, with RS facing and left-hand needle, *pick up 1 st from top edge of Cowl. Slide 4 sts over to opposite end of needle. Bring yarn around to back of work, K2. K2togtbl. Rep from * around top edge of Cowl.

Final row: Sl1. K2tog. psso. Fasten off. Sew beg and end of Applied I-Cord tog.

FINISHING

Bottom Edge Applied I-Cord

With A and pair of double-pointed needles, cast on 3 sts onto right-hand needle. Beg at back of Cowl, with RS facing and left-hand needle, *pick up 1 st from lower edge of Cowl. Slide 4 sts over to opposite end of needle. Bring yarn around to back of work, K2. K2togtbl. Rep from * around bottom edge and split of Cowl.

Final row: Sl1. K2tog. Psso. Fasten off. Sew beg and end of Applied I-Cord tog.•

WORK SOCK SCARF

MEASUREMENTS

Approx 8 x 90"/20.5 x 228.5cm

MATERIALS

Yarn

Bernat® Super Value™, 7oz/197g skeins, each approx 440yd/402m (acrylic)

• 2 skeins in #53044 True Gray (MC)

• 1 skein each in #07407 Winter White (A) and #00607 Berry (B)

Needles

• Size 8 (5mm) needles, *or size to obtain gauge*

GAUGE

18 sts and 24 rows = 4"/10cm in stockinette st using size 8 (5mm) needles.

TAKE TIME TO CHECK GAUGE.

STRIPE PATTERN

With A, work 12 rows.

With B, work 6 rows.

With A, work 12 rows.

These 30 rows form Stripe Pat.

SCARF

With A, cast on 57 sts.

1st row (RS): Sl1P. K2. *P3. K3. Rep from * to end of row.

2nd row: Sl1P. P2. *K3. P3. Rep from * to end of row.

These 2 rows form Rib Pat. First 2 rows of Stripe Pat are now complete.

Cont in Rib Pat, keeping cont of Stripe Pat, until all 30 rows of Stripe Pat are complete.

Break A. Join MC.

Cont in Rib Pat with MC only until Scarf from beg measures 85"/216cm, ending on a WS row.

Break MC. Join A.

Cont in Rib Pat and work 30 rows of Stripe Pat once more.

Cast off in Rib Pat.•

SEED STITCH PILLOW

Basic

MEASUREMENTS
Approx 24"/61cm square

MATERIALS

Yarn 🔟
Patons® Classic Wool Roving™, 3½oz/100g skeins, each approx 120yd/109m (wool)

Version 1
• 9 skeins in #77008 Aran OR #77309 Frosted Plum

Version 2
• 5 skeins each in #77008 Aran (A) and #77309 Frosted Plum (B)

Needles
• Size 10½ (6.5mm) knitting needles, *or size needed to obtain gauge*

GAUGE
9 sts and 12 rows = 4"/10cm in Seed St Pat with 2 strands held tog using size 10½ (6.5mm) needles. *TAKE TIME TO CHECK GAUGE.*

PILLOW

Front
Version 1 only: With 2 strands held together, cast on 54 sts.
Version 2 only: With 1 strand each of A and B held tog, cast on 54 sts.

All Versions:
1st row (RS): *K1. P1. Repeat from * to end of row.
2nd row: *P1. K1. Rep from * to end of row.
These 2 rows form Seed Stitch Pattern.
Cont in pat until work from beg measures approx 24"/61cm. Cast off.

Back (make 2 pieces alike)
Version 1 only: With 2 strands held tog, cast on 54 sts.
Version 2 only: With 1 strand each of A and B held tog, cast on 54 sts.

All Versions:
!st row (RS): *K2. P2. Rep from * to last 2 sts. K2.
2nd row: *P2. K2. Rep from * to last 2 sts. P2.
Rep last 2 rows twice more (6 rows total).

Proceed in Seed Stitch Pat as given for Front until work from beg measures 14"/35.5cm. Cast off.

FINISHING
Pin pieces to measurements. Cover with a damp cloth, leaving cloth to dry.
Overlap Back pieces to match Front, with ribbed sections in center to create opening to insert pillow form. Sew outer edge seams.•

MARL STRIPE KNIT SUPER SCARF

● ● ●

Intemediate

MEASUREMENTS

Approx 11 x 116"/28 x 295cm, excluding fringe

MATERIALS

Yarn ④

Patons® Classic Wool Worsted™, 3½oz/100g skeins, each approx 210yd/192m (wool)
- 4 skeins in #77215 Heath Heather (MC)
- 1 skein in #00229 Natural Mix (A)
- 2 skeins each in #77747 Claret (B), #77756 Honey (C), and #77768 Rich Teal (D)

Needles
- Size 11 (8mm) knitting needles, *or size needed to obtain gauge*

GAUGE

12 sts and 24 rows = 4"/10cm in Brioche Stitch with 2 strands of yarn held together and size 11 (8mm) needles. *TAKE TIME TO CHECK GAUGE*

SCARF

Stripe Pat

With 2 strands of MC, work 24 rows.

With 1 strand each of MC and A, work 24 rows.

With 2 strands of B, work 24 rows.

With 1 strand each of MC and B, work 24 rows.

With 2 strands of C, work 24 rows.

With 1 strand each of MC and C, work 24 rows.

With 2 strands of D, work 24 rows.

With 1 strand each of MC and D, work 24 rows.

These 192 rows form Stripe Pat.

With 2 strands of MC, cast on 33 sts.

1st row (RS): Sl1Pwyib. *Sl1Pwyif. yo (yo will lay across st). K1. Rep from * to end of row.

2nd row: Sl1Pwyib. K2tog (knit st and yo from previous row). *Sl1Pwyif. yo. K2tog. Rep from * to last st. K1.

3rd row: Sl1Pwyib. *Sl1Pwyif. yo. K2tog. Rep from * to last 2 sts. Sl1Pwyif. yo. K1. First 3 rows of Stripe Pat are complete. Rep last 2 rows for Brioche St Pat.

Cont in pat as established until work from beg measures approx. 116"/295cm, ending on a 23rd row of any stripe. Cast off. (WS).

FINISHING

Fringe

Cut lengths of all shades 30"/76cm long. Taking 4 strands of any 4 shades tog, fold in half and knot into fringe across each end of Scarf. Trim fringe evenly.●

TURNING POINTS KNIT BLANKET

Easy

MEASUREMENTS

Approx 52 x 62"/132 x 157.5cm

MATERIALS

Yarn (4)

Caron® One Pound™, 16oz/453.6g skeins, each approx 812yd/742m (acrylic)
• 2 skeins in #10589 Cream (MC)
• 1 skein each in #10535 Country Rose (A), #10621 Dark Pink (B), and #10516 Scarlet (C)

Needles

• Size 8 (5mm) knitting needles, *or size needed to obtain gauges*
• Size 8 (5mm) circular knitting needle 40"/101.5cm long

Notion

• Stitch marker

GAUGES

• 16 sts and 28 rows = 4"/10cm in garter st using size 8 (5mm) needles.
• Motif = Approx 10"/25.5cm square.
TAKE TIME TO CHECK GAUGES.

BLANKET

Motif

Make 10 with A as Color 2.
Make 10 with B as Color 2.
Make 10 with C as Color 2.

Note: It may be helpful to place a removable st marker on RS of work to keep track of RS and WS.
With MC and pair of needles, cast on 3 sts.
1st row (RS): Knit.
2nd row: Kfb. Knit to end of row.
Rep last row, inc 1 st at beg of every row to 56 sts, ending on a WS row.
Break MC.
Next row: With Color 2, K1. K2tog. Knit to end of row.
Rep last row to 3 sts.
Next row: K3tog.
Fasten off.

FINISHING

Sew Motifs tog as shown in photo, using a flat seam.

Border

With RS facing, MC, and circular needle, pick up and knit 240 sts evenly along side edge of Blanket.
Do *not* join. Working back and forth across needle in rows, proceed as follows:
Knit 4 rows.
Cast off knitwise (WS).
Rep for opposite side edge of Blanket.
With RS facing, MC and circular needle, pick up and knit 206 sts evenly along top edge of Blanket.
Do *not* join. Working back and forth across needle in rows, proceed as follows:
Knit 4 rows.
Cast off knitwise (WS).
Rep for bottom edge of Blanket.●

COZY CABLE HAT

SIZE

One size to fit average Adult.

MATERIALS

Yarn

Bernat® Softee® Chunky™, 3½oz/100g skeins, each approx 108 yd/99m (acrylic)

• 2 skeins in #28048 Taupe Gray

Needles

• Set of 4 size 10½ (6.5mm) double-pointed needles (dpn), *or size needed to obtain gauge*
• Set of 4 size 11 (8mm) double-pointed knitting needles *or size needed to obtain gauge*

Notions

• Cable needle
• Stitch marker

GAUGE

11 sts and 14 rows = 4"/10cm in stockinette st using larger needles. *TAKE TIME TO CHECK GAUGE*

HAT

With smaller set of needles, cast on 60 sts. Divide sts on 3 needles and join in rnd, taking care not to twist sts and placing a marker on first st.

1st rnd: *K2. P2. Rep from * around.

Rep last rnd (K2. P2) ribbing for 4"/10cm.

Change to larger set of needles and proceed as follows:

Next rnd: *K4. Kfb. Rep from * around. 72 sts.

Proceed in Cable Pat as follows:

1st and 2nd rnds: *K8. P4. Rep from * around.

3rd rnd: *C4B. C4F. P4. Rep from * around.

4th rnd: As 1st rnd.

These 4 rnds form Cable Pat.

Cont in Cable Pat until work from beg measures approx 10"/25.5cm, ending on a 4th rnd.

Shape crown

1st rnd: *Ssk. K4. K2tog. P4. Rep from * around. 60 sts.

2nd rnd: *K6. P4. Rep from * around.

3rd rnd: *C3B. C3F. (P2tog) twice. Rep from * around. 48 sts

4th rnd: *K6. P2. Rep from * around.

5th rnd: *Ssk. K2. K2tog. P2. Rep from * around. 36 sts.

6th rnd: *K4. P2. Rep from * around.

7th rnd: *Ssk. K2tog. P2tog. Rep from * around. 18 sts. Break yarn, leaving a long end. Draw end tightly through rem sts and fasten securely.

FINISHING

Pompom

Wind yarn around 4 fingers approx 80 times. Remove from fingers and tie tightly in center. Cut through each side of loops. Trim to a smooth round shape, approx 4"/10cm in diameter. Sew to top of Hat.●

MINIMALIST JACKET

SIZES

XS/S (M, L, XL, 2/3XL, 4/5XL)

MEASUREMENTS

To fit bust measurement 28-34 (36-38, 40-42, 44-46, 48-54, 56-62)"/71-86.5 (91.5-96.5, 101.5-106.5, 112-117, 122-137, 142-157.5)cm

Finished bust measurement 44 (48, 52, 56, 60, 64)"/112 (122, 132, 142, 152.5, 162.5)cm

MATERIALS

Yarn (6)

Bernat® Softee® Chunky™, 3½oz/100g skeins, each approx. 108yd/99m (acrylic)

• 10 (11, 12, 13, 14, 15) skeins in #28219 Seagreen

Needles

• Size 11 (8 mm) circular knitting needle 40"/101.5cm long, *or size needed to obtain gauge*

Notions

• Spare needle

• Stitch marker

GAUGE

10 sts and 28 rows = 4"/10cm in garter st using size 11 (8 mm) needles.

TAKE TIME TO CHECK GAUGE.

JACKET

Note: Jacket is worked sideways in one piece from cuff to cuff.

Beg at Left Sleeve, cast on 4 sts. Work i-cord cast on as follows:

1st row: Knit. Slip 4 sts just knit back onto left-hand needle.

2nd row: Inc 1 st in first st. Knit to end of row.

Slip 4 sts just knit back onto left-hand needle. (1 st increased).

Rep last row until there are 44 (44, 46, 46, 50, 52) sts.

Next row: Slip last 3 sts just knit back onto left-hand

needle. K2tog. K1. Slip last 2 sts back onto left-hand needle. K2tog. 42 (42, 46, 46, 48, 50) sts.

Cont in garter st (knit every row), noting first row is WS until work from beg measures 8½ (8, 8, 7¼, 7, 6¼)"/21.5 (20.5, 20.5, 18.5, 18, 16)cm, ending on a WS row.

Shape Back and Front

Cast on 60 (60, 62, 62, 64, 64) sts at beg of next 2 rows. 162 (162, 170, 170, 176, 178) sts.

Cont even in garter st until work from last cast on row measures 7½ (8½, 9¼, 10¼, 11, 12)"/19 (21.5, 23.5, 26, 28, 30.5)cm, ending on a WS row.

Divide for Neck

1st row (RS): K78 (78, 82, 82, 85, 86) and place on spare needle for Back. Cast off 8 sts for neck. Knit to end of row. 76 (76, 80, 80, 83, 84) sts.

Knit 9 rows even.

Shape left neck

Next row (RS): K2. ssk. Knit to end of row.

Knit 5 rows even.

Next row: K2. ssk. Knit to end of row.

Knit 3 rows even.

Next row: K2. ssk. Knit to end of row.

Rep last 4 rows once more.

Next row: Knit.

Sizes 2/3XL and 4/5XL only

Next row: K2. ssk. Knit to end of row.

Next row: Knit.

All sizes

Next row (RS): K2. ssk. Knit to end of row.

Next row: Knit to last 4 sts. K2tog. K2.

Rep last 2 rows 0 (0, 1, 1, 1, 1) time more.

Cast off rem 70 (70, 72, 72, 74, 75) sts.

With WS facing, join yarn to 78 (78, 82, 82, 85, 86) sts on spare needle for Back. Cont in garter st until work from join measures 7 (7, 7½, 7½, 8, 8)"/18 (18, 19, 19, 20.5,

MINIMALIST JACKET

20.5)cm, ending on a RS row. Place sts on spare needle.

Right Front

Cast on 70 (70, 72, 72, 74, 75) sts.

Shape right neck

Next row (RS): K2. M1. Knit to end of row.

Next row: Knit to last 2 sts. M1. K1.

Rep last 2 rows 0 (0, 1, 1, 1, 1) time more. 72 (72, 76, 76, 78, 79) sts.

Sizes 2/3XL and 4/5XL only

Next row: K2. M1. Knit to end of row.

Next row: Knit.

All sizes

Next row (RS): K2. M1. Knit to end of row.

Knit 3 rows even.

Next row: K2. M1. Knit to end of row.

Rep last 4 rows once more.

Knit 5 rows even.

Next row: K2. M1. Knit to end of row. 76 (76, 80, 80, 83, 84) sts.

Knit 10 rows even.

Join Back and Front

Next row (WS): K76 (76, 80, 80, 83, 84). Cast on 8 sts. K78 (78, 82, 82, 85, 86) across Back sts from spare needle. 162 (162, 170, 170, 176, 178) sts. Place marker at end of last row.

Cont in garter st until work from marker measures 7½ (8½, 9¼, 10¼, 11, 12)"/19 (21.5, 23.5, 26, 26, 30.5)cm, end on a RS row.

Divide for Right Sleeve

Cast off 60 (60, 62, 62, 64, 64) sts at beg of next 2 rows. 42 (42,

46, 46, 48,-50) sts.

Cont in garter st until Right Sleeve measures 8½ (8, 8, 7¼, 7, 6¼)"/21.5 (20.5, 20.5, 18.5, 18, 16)cm, ending on a RS row.

I-cord cast off

Cast on 3 sts onto end of left-hand needle. *K2. K2tog. Slip last 3 sts back onto left-hand needle. Rep from * until 3 sts rem. K2tog. K1. Slip last 2 sts onto end of left-hand needle. K2tog. Fasten off.

FINISHING

Sew side and underarm seams.

Applied i-cord edging

With RS facing, beg at Left Front, pick up and knit 110 (120, 130, 140, 150, 160) sts along bottom edge of Jacket. Break yarn.

Cast on 2 sts. K2, then knit first picked up st on bottom edge. Slip last 3 sts onto left-hand needle. *K2. K2togtbl. Slip last 3 sts onto left-hand needle. Rep from * until 3 sts rem. K2tog. K1. Slip last 2 sts onto end of left-hand needle. K2tog. Fasten off.

With RS facing and beg at bottom Right Front, pick up and knit 88 (88, 92, 92, 95, 97) sts up Right Front edge to neck shaping, 62 (62, 68, 68, 74, 74) sts to beg of Left Front neck shaping and 88 (88, 92, 92, 95, 97) sts down Left Front edge. 238 (238, 252, 252, 264, 268) sts. Break yarn.

Cast on 2 sts. K2, then knit first picked up st on Right Front. Slip last 3 sts onto left-hand needle. *K2. K2togtbl. Slip last 3 sts onto left-hand needle. Rep from * until 3 sts rem. K2tog. K1. Slip last 2 sts onto end of left-hand needle. K2tog. Fasten off.•

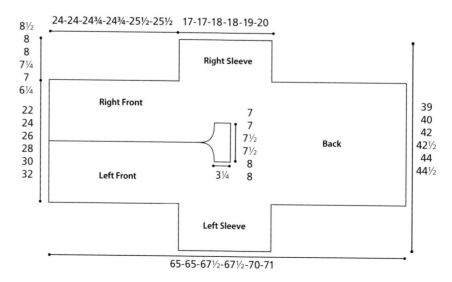

Easy

MEASUREMENT

Approx 20"/51cm square

MATERIALS

Yarn 4

Bernat® Handicrafter Cotton®, 14oz/400g skeins, each approx 710yd/650m (cotton)
• 1 skein each in #00002 Off White and #27215 Robins Egg

Bernat® Handicrafter Cotton®, 1¾oz/50g skeins, each approx 84yd/77m (cotton)
• 8 skeins in #01699 Tangerine

Needles

• Size 7 (4.5mm) knitting needles, *or size needed to obtain gauge*

Notion

• 20"/51cm square pillow form.

GAUGE

20 sts and 26 rows = 4"/10cm in stockinette st using size 7 (4.5mm) needles.
TAKE TIME TO CHECK GAUGE.

PILLOWS

FRONT and BACK (Make alike)

Cast on 101 sts.

1st row (RS): K1. P1. *yo. P2tog. P6. Rep from * to last 3 sts. yo. P2tog. K1.

2nd, 4th, and 6th rows: K2. P1. *K7. P1. Rep from * to last 2 sts. K2.

3rd, 5th, and 7th rows: K1. P1. *K1. P7. Rep from * to last 3 sts. K1. P1. K1.

8th row: K1. Purl to last st. K1.

9th row: K1. P5. *yo. P2tog. P6. Rep from * to last 7 sts. yo. P2tog. P4. K1.

10th, 12th, and 14th rows: K6. P1. *K7. P1. Rep from * to last 6 sts. K6.

11th, 13th, and 15th rows: K1. P5. *K1. P7. Rep from * to last 7 sts. K1. P5. K1.

16th row: K1. Purl to last st. K1.

These 16 rows form pat.

Cont in pat until work from beg measures approx 20"/51cm, ending on an 8th or 16th row of pat.

Cast off.

FINISHING

Sew 3 sides of Front and Back tog. Insert pillow form. Sew rem side closed.•

EASY-GOING KNIT PULLOVER

Easy

SIZES
XS/S (M, L, XL, 2/3XL, 4/5XL).

MEASUREMENTS
To fit bust measurement 28-34 (36-38, 40-42, 44-46, 48-54, 56-62)"/71-86.5 (91.5-96.5, 101.5-106.5, 112-117, 122-137, 142-157.5)cm

Finished bust measurement 41 (44, 48, 52, 60, 64)"/104 (112, 122, 132, 152.5, 162.5)cm

MATERIALS
Yarn (5)

Bernat® Roving, 3½oz/100g skeins, each approx. 120yd/109m (acrylic/wool)
• 8 (9, 10, 11, 13, 15) skeins in #00071 Plum

Needles
• Size 10½ (6.5 mm) knitting needles, *or size needed to obtain gauge*

Notions
• 2 stitch holders
• Stitch markers

GAUGE
12 sts and 16 rows = 4"/10cm in Texture Pat using size 10½ (6.5 mm) needles
TAKE TIME TO CHECK GAUGE.

NOTE
The instructions are written for smallest size. If changes are necessary for larger size(s) the instructions will be written thus ( ). When only one number for each size is given, it applies to all sizes.

PULLOVER
Back
**Cast on 63 (67, 73, 79, 91, 97) sts.

1st row (RS): *K1tbl. P1. Rep from * to last st. K1tbl.
2nd row: *P1tbl. K1. Rep from * to last st. P1tbl.
Rep last 2 rows of twisted ribbing for 2"/5cm, ending on a 2nd row.

Proceed in Texture Pat as follows:
1st row (RS): Knit.
2nd row: K1. *K1below. P1. Rep from * to last 2 sts. K1below. K1.
3rd row: Knit.
4th row: Purl.
These 4 rows form Texture Pat.

Cont in pat until work from beg measures 19"/48cm, ending on a WS row.

Shape armholes
Keeping cont of pat, cast off 4 sts at beg of next 2 rows. 55 (59, 65, 71, 83, 89) sts.**
Cont even in pat until armhole measures 8 (9, 9½, 10, 10, 10½)"/20.5 (23, 24.5, 25.5, 25.5, 27.5)cm, ending on a WS row.

Shape shoulders
Keeping cont of pat, cast off 7 (8, 9, 10, 13, 15) sts beg next 2 rows, then 7 (8, 9, 11, 14, 15) sts beg following 2 rows. Leave rem 27 (27, 29, 29, 29, 29) sts on a st holder.

Front
Work from ** to ** as given for Back.
Cont even in pat until armhole measures 5 (6, 6½, 7, 7, 7½)"/12.5 (15, 16.5, 18, 18, 19.5)cm, end on a WS row.

Shape neck
Next row (RS): Pat across 20 (22, 24, 27, 33, 36) sts (neck edge). Turn. Leave rem sts on a spare needle.
Cont in pat, dec 1 st at neck edge on next 4 rows, then

EASY-GOING KNIT PULLOVER

on following RS rows twice more. 14 (16, 18, 21, 27, 30) sts.
Cont even in pat until armhole measures same length as Back to shoulder, ending on a WS row.

Shape shoulder

Keeping cont of pat, cast off 7 (8, 9, 10, 13, 15) sts beg next row.
Work 1 row even. Cast off rem 7 (8, 9, 11, 14, 15) sts.

With RS facing, slip next 15 (15, 17, 17, 17, 17) sts onto a st holder. Rejoin yarn to rem sts and pat to end of row.
Cont in pat, dec 1 st at neck edge on next 4 rows, then on following RS rows twice more. 14 (16, 18, 21, 27, 30) sts.
Cont even in pat until armhole measures same length as Back to shoulder, ending on a RS row.

Shape shoulder

Keeping cont of pat, cast off 7 (8, 9, 10, 13, 15) sts beg next row.
Work 1 row even. Cast off rem 7 (8, 9, 11, 14, 15) sts.

Sleeves

Cast on 33 (33, 33, 35, 37, 39) sts.
Work 2"/5cm in twisted ribbing as given for Back, ending on a 2nd row.

Proceed in Texture Pat as given for Back for 4 rows.
Keeping cont of pat (as placed in last 4 rows), inc 1 st each end of next and following 6th (6th, 6th, 4th, 4th, 4th) rows until there are 49 (45, 45, 61, 61, 63) sts, taking inc sts into pat.

Sizes M and L only: Inc 1 st each end of following 4th rows until there are (55, 57) sts, taking inc sts into pat.

All sizes: Cont even in pat until Sleeve from beg measures 18 (18, 17, 17, 16, 16)"/45.5 (45.5, 43, 43, 40.5, 40.5)cm, ending on a WS row. Place markers at each end of last row.
Work 4 rows even in pat.
Cast off.

FINISHING

Collar

Sew right shoulder seam. With RS facing, pick up and knit 12 sts down left front neck edge. K15 (15, 17, 17, 17, 17) from Front st holder. Pick up and knit 12 sts up right front neck edge. K27 (27, 29, 29, 29, 29) from Back st holder, inc 1 st at center. 67 (67, 71, 71, 71, 71) sts.

Next row (WS): Purl.

Beg on a 1st row, work in Texture Pat as given for Back until Collar measures approx 7½"/19cm, ending on a 2nd row of pat. Cast off knitwise loosely.
Sew left shoulder and Collar seam.

Sew in sleeves placing rows above markers along cast off sts of Front and Back to form square armholes. Sew side and sleeve seams.•

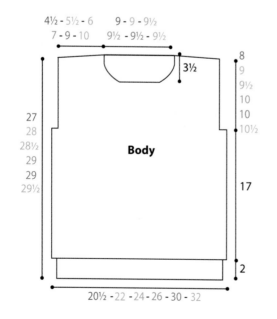

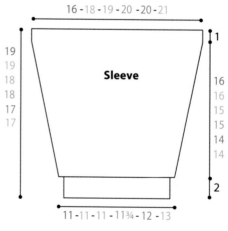

SUBTLE LEAVES SHAWL

Intermediate

MEASUREMENTS
Approx 50"/127cm wide x 18"/45.5cm deep

MATERIALS
Yarn
Patons® Silk Bamboo™, 2.2oz/65g balls, each approx 102yd/93m (bamboo/silk)
• 4 balls in #85416 Blush

Needles
• Size 6 (4mm) circular knitting needle 36"/91.5cm long, *or size needed to obtain gauge*

Notion
• Stitch marker

GAUGE
22 sts and 28 rows = 4"/10cm in stockinette st using size 6 (4mm) needles.
TAKE TIME TO CHECK GAUGE.

SHAWL
Cast on 9 sts. Do not join. Working back and forth across needle in rows, proceed as follows:

1st row (RS): K2. yo. K2. M1. PM. K1. M1. K2. yo. K2. 13 sts.

2nd row: K2. Purl to last 2 sts. K2.

3rd row: K2. yo. Knit to marker. M1. K1. M1. Knit to last 2 sts. yo. K2. 17 sts.

Rep last 2 rows, inc 4 sts each RS row, until there are 189 sts, ending on a WS row.

Proceed in Leaf Lace Pat (see Chart I):

1st row (RS): K2. yo. K2. *ssk. yo. K1. yo. K2tog. K11. Rep from * to last 9 sts. ssk. yo. K1. yo. K2tog. K2. yo. K2.

2nd row: K2. yo. P2. *P2tog. P1. yo. P1. yo. P1. P2togtbl. P9. Rep from * to last 11 sts. P2tog. P1. yo. P1. yo. P1. P2togtbl. P2. yo. K2.

3rd row: K2. yo. K2. *ssk. K2. yo. K1. yo. K2. K2tog. K7. Rep from * to last 13 sts. ssk. K2. yo. K1. yo. K2. K2tog. K2. yo. K2.

4th row: K2. yo. P2. *P2tog. P3. yo. P1. yo. P3. P2togtbl. P5. Rep from * to last 15 sts. P2tog. P3. yo. P1. yo. P3. P2togtbl. P2. yo. K2.

5th row: K2. yo. K2. *ssk. K4. yo. K1. yo. K4. K2tog. K3. Rep from * to last 17 sts. ssk. K4. yo. K1. yo. K4. K2tog. K2. yo. K2.

6th row: K2. yo. Purl to last 2 sts. yo. K2.

7th row: K2. yo. Knit to last 2 sts. yo. K2.

8th row: As 6th row.

Rep 1st to 8th rows twice more. 237 sts.

SUBTLE LEAVES SHAWL

FINISHING

Border: 1st to 5th rows

Work 1st to 5th rows of Leaf Lace Pat (see Chart II). 247 sts.

6th row (WS): K2. yo. K9. *yo. K1. yo. K15. Rep from * to last 12 sts. yo. K1. yo. K9. yo. K2.

7th row: K2. yo. K11. *yo. K1. yo. K17. Rep from * to last 14 sts. yo. K1. yo. K11. yo. K2.

8th row: K2. yo. K13. *yo. K1. yo. K19. Rep from * to last 16 sts. yo. K1. yo. K13. Yo. K2.

9th row: K2. yo. K15. *yo. K1. yo. K21. Rep from * to last 18 sts. yo. K1. yo. K15. yo. K2.

Cast off loosely.

Key

☐ = Knit on RS rows; Purl on WS rows

⊟ = Purl on RS rows; Knit on WS rows.

⊡ = yo

◿ = K2tog

⊠ = P2tog

◣ = ssk

⊠ = P2togtbl

Chart I - Leaf Lace Pat

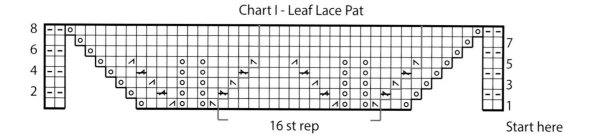

16 st rep

Start here

Chart II - Border Pat

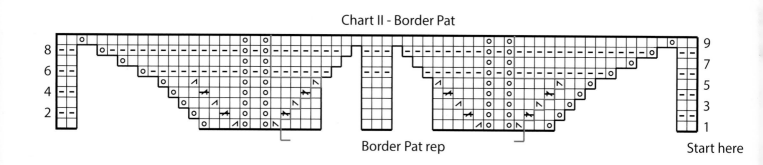

Border Pat rep

Start here

SLEEVELESS KNIT TURTLENECK

Easy

SIZES
XS/S (M, L, XL, 2/3XL, 4/5XL)

MEASUREMENTS
To fit bust measurement 28-34 (36-38, 40-42, 44-46, 48-54, 56-62)"/71-86.5 (91.5-96.5, 101.5-106.5, 112-117, 122-137, 142-157.5)cm

Finished bust measurement 36 (40, 44, 48, 57, 65)"/91.5 (101.5, 112, 122, 144.5, 165)cm

MATERIALS
Yarn (5)
Patons® Alpaca Blend™, 3½oz/100g skeins, each approx. 155yd/142m (acrylic/wool/nylon/alpaca)
• 3 (3, 3, 4, 4, 5) skeins in #01005 Slate

Needles
• Size 10 (6mm) knitting needles, *or size needed to obtain gauge*

Notions
• 2 stitch holders
• 1 stitch marker

GAUGE
15 sts and 20 rows = 4"/10cm in stockinette st using size 10 (6mm) needles.
TAKE TIME TO CHECK GAUGE.

TURTLENECK
Note: The instructions are written for smallest size. If changes are necessary for larger size(s) the instructions will be written thus ( ). When only one number is given, it applies to all sizes.

BACK
Note: Back is approx 1"/2.5cm longer than Front.
Cast on 67 (75, 83, 91, 107, 123) sts.
1st row (RS): *K3. P1. Rep from * to last 3 sts. K3.

2nd row: *P3. K1. Rep from * to last 3 sts. P3.**
Rep last 2 rows (K3. P1) ribbing 6 times more.
Proceed as follows:

1st row (RS): Knit.
2nd row: K5. Purl to last 5 sts. K5.
Rep last 2 rows until work from beg measures 16 (16, 17, 17, 18, 19)"/40.5 (40.5, 43, 43, 45.5, 48cm), ending on a WS row.

Armhole Shaping
Cast off 3 (6, 7, 8, 9, 10) sts beg next 2 rows. 61 (63, 69, 75, 89, 103) sts.

Size 4/5XL only
Cast off 3 sts beg next 2 rows. 97 sts.

Sizes 2/3XL and 4/5XL only
1st row (RS): Sl1. K1. ssk. Knit to last 4 sts. K2tog. K2. (87, 95) sts.
2nd row: Sl1P. P1. P2tog. Purl to last 4 sts. P2togtbl. P2. (85, 93) sts.
Rep last 2 rows (4, 5) times more. (69, 73) sts.

All sizes
1st row (RS): Sl1. K1. ssk. Knit to last 4 sts. K2tog. K2. 59 (61, 67, 73, 67, 75) sts.
2nd row: Sl1P. Purl to end of row. Rep last 2 rows 6 (7, 7, 9, 4, 4) times more. 47 (47, 53, 55, 59, 65) sts.
Cont even in stockinette st, slipping first st of each row until armholes measure 6 (6½, 6½, 7, 7, 7½)"/15 (16.5, 16.5, 18, 18, 19)cm, ending on a WS row.

Shape shoulders
Cast off 5 (5, 6, 6, 7, 8) sts beg next 2 rows, then 4 (4, 5, 5, 6, 7) sts beg next 2 rows. Place rem 29 (29, 31, 33, 33, 35) sts onto a st holder.

Front
Work from ** to ** as given for Back. Rep last 2 rows (K3. P1) ribbing 3 times more.
Proceed as follows:

SLEEVELESS KNIT TURTLENECK

1st row (RS): Knit.

2nd row: K5. Purl to last 5 sts. K5. Rep last 2 rows until work from beg measures 15 (15, 16, 16, 17, 18)"/38 (38, 40.5, 40.5, 43, 45.5)cm, ending on a WS row.

Armhole Shaping

Cast off 3 (6, 7, 8, 9, 11) sts beg next 2 rows. 61 (63, 69, 75, 89, 101) sts.

Sizes 2/3XL and 4/5XL only

1st row (RS): Sl1. K1. ssk. Knit to last 4 sts. K2tog. K2. (87, 99) sts.

2nd row: Sl1P. P1. P2tog. Purl to last 4 sts. P2togtbl. P2. Rep last 2 rows (4, 5) times more. (69, 65) sts.

All sizes

1st row (RS): Sl1. K1. ssk. Knit to last 4 sts. K2tog. K2. 59 (61, 67, 73, 67, 63) sts.

2nd row: Sl1P. Purl to end of row. Rep last 2 rows 6 (7, 7, 9, 4, 5) times more. 47 (47, 53, 55, 59, 65) sts. Cont even in stockinette st, slipping first st of each row until armhole measures approx 4¼ (4¾, 4¾, 5¼, 5¼, 5¾)"/11 (12, 12, 13, 13, 14.5)cm, ending on a WS row.

Neck shaping

1st row: Sl1. K13 (13, 15, 15, 17, 19). K2tog. Turn. Leave rem 31 (31, 35, 37, 39, 43) sts on spare needle.

2nd row: P2tog. Purl to end of row.

3rd row: Sl1. Knit to last 2 sts. K2tog. Rep last 2 rows to 9 (9, 11, 11, 13, 15) sts. Work 1 row even.

Shape Shoulder

Cast off 5 (5, 6, 6, 7, 8) sts beg next row. Work 1 row even. Cast off rem 4 (4, 5, 5, 6, 7) sts.

With RS facing, slip next 15 (15, 17, 19, 19, 21) sts onto a st holder. Join yarn to rem sts. ssk. Knit to end of row. 15 (15, 17, 17, 19, 21) sts.

Next row: Sl1P. Purl to last 2 sts. P2togtbl.

Next row: ssk. Knit to end of row. Rep last 2 rows to 9 (9, 11, 11, 13, 15) sts. Work 2 rows even.

Shape shoulder

Cast off 5 (5, 6, 6, 7, 8) sts beg next row. Work 1 row even. Cast off rem 4 (4, 5, 5, 6, 7) sts.

FINISHING

Sew shoulder seams. Sew side seams from armhole to top of ribbing leaving sides of ribbing open.

Collar

With RS facing and circular needle, beg at right shoulder, pick up and knit 9 sts down right front neck edge. K15 (15, 17, 19, 19, 21) from Front st holder. Pick up and knit 9 sts up left front neck edge. K29 (29, 31, 33, 33, 35) from Back neck st holder, dec 2 (2, 0, 1, 1, 2) st(s) evenly across. 60 (60, 66, 69, 69, 72) sts. PM. Join to beg working in rnd.

1st rnd: *K2. P1. Rep from * around.

Rep last rnd until Collar measures 4"/10cm.

Cast off loosely in pat.●

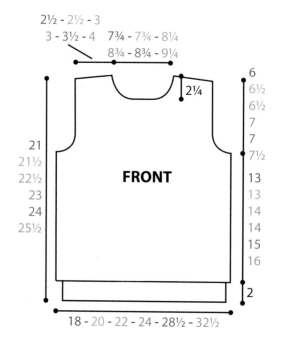

2½ - 2½ - 3
3 - 3½ - 4   7¾ - 7¾ - 8¼
8¾ - 8¾ - 9¼

2¼

FRONT

21
21½
22½
23
24
25½

6
6½
6½
7
7
7½
13
13
14
14
15
16
2

18 - 20 - 22 - 24 - 28½ - 32½

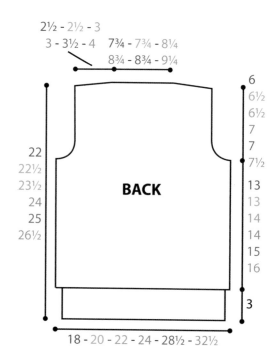

2½ - 2½ - 3
3 - 3½ - 4   7¾ - 7¾ - 8¼
8¾ - 8¾ - 9¼

BACK

22
22½
23½
24
25
26½

6
6½
6½
7
7
7½
13
13
14
14
15
16
3

18 - 20 - 22 - 24 - 28½ - 32½